G000151956

ZEN

ZEN

Edited by
Randy Burgess

Ariel Books

Andrews and McMeel
Kansas City

ISBN: 0-8362-3132-5

Library of Congress Catalog Card Number: 95-60377

CONTENTS

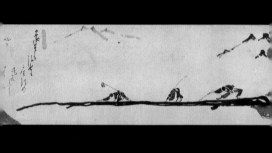

ZEN

INTRODUCTION

Zen. Merely to say the word is to feel its strange attraction—a single syllable that starts with a buzz and then snaps shut, like a box with a secret inside. To some of us, this ancient religion may appear mystical, baffling. The incense of the Orient stings our nostrils, and we imagine black-robed, frowning monks with shaved heads, seated in long rows, as silent as the dust.

To others, Zen may seem more familiar. From an overheard conversation or from a glance through an intriguing book, we may consider it not so much a religion as a philosophy, a way of waking to the present moment. Maybe we've even tried a little everyday Zen—doing something as ordinary as washing the dishes but paying absolute attention, deliberately emptying our mind, not thinking about taxes or the mortgage or anything else. With all the troubles in our modern world, such restful simplicity is appealing. Both images are true. Both are Zen.

This small book seeks to capture just a little of the essence of this religion—like casting a single drop of water into a ravine, as a scholar said centuries ago in China. Read on. Unlike the way things happen in legend, you won't necessarily become enlightened on the spot—but you may well be startled or amused. In Zen, that is often the first step.

•

Even a worm an inch long has a
soul half an inch long.
    —*Buddhist proverb*

ZEN

THE ROOTS
OF ZEN

*Never let go the
reins of the wild colt
of the heart.*
—Buddhist proverb

Since Zen is a form of Buddhism, its origins go back to the Gautama Buddha himself, born the son of a king and queen in 563 B.C. Rejecting his heritage of aristocratic luxury, this young man wandered India for six years, seeking the truth about human pain and suffering. One night, while meditating under a banyan tree, he found enlightenment. In Zen, as in other forms of Buddhism, enlightenment is a liberation from ego, desire, and suffering. The divisions between self and world and life and death are seen for what they are: illusion. The true self is emptiness.

Zen, called *Ch'an* in Chinese, wasn't officially founded as a separate branch of Buddhism until the sixth century, when an Indian monk named Bodhidharma traveled to China. Bodhidharma decided that meditation, not the study of scripture or the worship of images, was the best way to reach enlightenment. He began to teach this way to others. By the twelfth century such teachings reached Japan.

Like most religions, Zen has its

severe side: it's nothing to fool around with, not if you want to learn the secret of life and death. At least, that's what the legends say. For instance, when Bodhidharma first arrived in China, a man called Hui-k'o came to him and begged to be his disciple. But Bodhidharma thought Hui-k'o wasn't determined enough and told him to go away. Day after day, Hui-k'o waited patiently outside Bodhidharma's dwelling, until the falling snow reached his knees. Still the master ignored him. Finally, to prove his resolve, Hui-k'o took a hatchet, hacked off his left arm, and offered it to the master. Even Bodhidharma was impressed.

Today, potential students no longer have to resort to such extremes. However, Morinaga Soko, a former kamikaze pilot who turned to Zen after World War II and later became a master, still tells the story of how he applied to a monastery and was forced to wait outside for days, shivering in the cold and suffering insults and kicks from the monks. The monks' reasons for this behavior, of course, were the same as Bodhidharma's: to test his resolve.

TWO PATHS TO ENLIGHTENMENT

To make things more confusing, at least for Westerners, there isn't one school of Zen, but many. The two largest schools are *Soto* and *Rinzai,* and each believes in a different path to enlightenment.

Soto teaches that enlightenment doesn't need to be gained so much as remembered. Seated meditation (*zazen*) and an attitude of nonseeking are the keys to this practice. If you do these things properly, you'll be acting like the buddha you already are.

Rinzai, on the other hand, warns

that supreme exertion is needed to awaken to the truth. We need to be shocked out of our conventional way of looking at things. This is accomplished through vigorous *zazen* and repeated meditation on a *koan*—familiar to many Westerners as a kind of mystic, intellectually unsolvable riddle, such as "What was your original face, the one before your parents were born?"

A little wisdom is a stumbling block on the way to Buddhahood.
—Buddhist proverb

ZEN

ZEN BY NUMBER

*In every speck of
dust are Buddhas
without number.*
—Anonymous

The Ten Grave Precepts

1. Not to kill
2. Not to steal
3. Not to misuse sex
4. Not to lie
5. Not to take drugs
6. Not to discuss the faults of others
7. Not to praise oneself while degrading others
8. Not to spare the teachings
9. Not to indulge in anger
10. Not to malign the Three Treasures

THE THREE TREASURES

1. The Buddha (enlightened being)
2. The Dharma (Buddhist teachings)
3. The Sangha (community of all beings)

THE FOUR NOBLE TRUTHS

1. Suffering is everywhere.
2. Suffering has a cause and an effect.
3. There is freedom from suffering.
4. Freedom is the Eightfold Path.

THE EIGHTFOLD PATH

1. Right understanding
2. Right thought
3. Right speech
4. Right action
5. Right livelihood
6. Right effort
7. Right attention
8. Right concentration

The Four Vows

These vows are recited every morning and evening by good Buddhists—especially by Zen monks:

I vow to save all sentient beings.
I vow to abandon avarice, hatred, and
  ignorance.
I vow to study the sacred teachings.
I vow to follow the way of the
  Buddha.

ZEN

BURN THIS
BOOK!

*The mouth is the
front-gate of all
misfortune.*
—Buddhist proverb

One of the many paradoxes in Zen is that while enlightenment can't be gained through a book, everybody seems to spend a lot of time reading just the same. Zen's must-read list over the centuries has included sacred Sanskrit texts called *sutras,* classical Chinese and Japanese literature, poetry, collections of koans, and essays by the masters.

Books have also played a big part in introducing Zen to the West, with Americans devouring such classics as Philip Kapleau's *The Three Pillars of Zen* and Alan Watts's *The Spirit of Zen,* along with such recent oddities as Robert Pirsig's *Zen and the Art of Motorcycle Maintenance*. Still, the heroes of Zen often seem to get fed up with all this reading.

In one story from ninth century China, Te-shan, a famous scholar, visits a Zen master called Lung-tan to discuss a particular sacred text. They talk all day long, until Te-shan's voice becomes hoarse and he's too worn out to keep arguing. He takes a look outside Lung-tan's hut.

"Hey," Te-shan says, "it's dark out." The master lights a candle for his guest—then abruptly blows it out. For some reason, this means so much to Te-shan that he instantly becomes enlightened.

And the next day he burns all his books.

To have some deep feeling about Buddhism is not the point; we just do what we should do, like eating supper and going to bed. This is Buddhism.
—*Shunryu Suzuki*

ZEN RIDDLES:
KOANS AND
ANECDOTES

*If you meet the
Buddha along the
road, kill him.
—Zen saying*

The literal meaning of koan is "public
case"—which makes sense, since
koans are recorded encounters, pre-
served through the centuries, between
clever masters and baffled students.
They're miniature vaudeville routines
about enlightenment, with the master
usually getting the punch line.

Like a good poem, a koan is contra-
dictory: it puts into words what can't
be put into words. D. T. Suzuki has
written, "On examination we notice at
once that there is no room in the koan
to insert an intellectual interpretation.

The knife is not sharp enough to cut the koan open and see what are its contents."

Traditionally, there are seventeen hundred koans, but only a handful are regularly studied. A sampling follows—with a few nontraditional examples added for good measure.

❧

Ummon said, "Look! The world is vast and wide. Why do you put on your priest's robe at the sound of the bell?"

❧

A monk asked Lung-ya, "What did old masters attain when they arrived at the ultimate stage?"

Lung-ya answered, "They were like burglars, sneaking into an empty house."

⌒ ·

One morning after a lecture to his monks, Yueh-shan was approached by one of them.

"I've got a problem," the monk confessed. "Can you solve it for me?"

Yueh-shan, looking wise, said, "I will solve it for you at tonight's lecture."

Satisfied, the monk went away.

That evening, when the monks assembled in the hall, Yueh-shan called out loudly, "The monk who told me this morning he had a problem—come up here immediately!"

Expectantly the monk came forward. The master rose and grabbed him roughly.

"Look here, monks," Yueh-shan said, "this fellow has a problem!" Pushing the monk aside, Yueh-shan returned to his room without giving any lecture at all.

Wei-shan was visiting his master Pai-chang one day, when the master abruptly pointed toward the fireplace and ordered him: "Dig into those ashes and see if there's any fire left."

Wei-shan hesitated, then got down on his hands and knees and made a half-hearted attempt at poking among the ashes.

"Nothing, sir," Wei-shan said.

At this Pai-chang got up, squatted beside Wei-shan, and dug his fingers down really deep into the ashes. After a moment he grunted with satisfaction and held up his hand: in his fingers he

ZEN

held a tiny coal, hot and glowing.
This awoke Wei-shan.

~

A student asked Chao-chou, "If all the
many things in the universe return to
One, to what does the One return?"

Chao-chou answered, "When I was
in Ch'ing Province I had a robe made
out of hemp. It weighed seven
pounds."

~

A monk asked Chao-chou, "Is there
Buddha-nature in a dog?"

Chao-chou said, "Mu!"

A monk came to Pai-chang and asked, "What's the most wonderful thing in the world?"

Pai-chang replied, "I sit on top of this mountain."

Impressed, the monk paid homage to the master, ceremonially folding his hands.

So, of course, Pai-chang hit the monk with his *kyosaku* (stick).

ANECDOTES

One day, Ikkyu received a visit from Murata-Shuko. Since Shuko was widely respected as a master of the tea ceremony and they were about to drink tea anyway, Ikkyu decided to ask Shuko what he thought of a particular koan—one that happened to involve tea drinking.

But Shuko didn't answer, keeping his mouth shut. At last, Ikkyu shrugged and served the tea. Just as Shuko was lifting his cup to his lips, Ikkyu cried out and smashed the cup with his iron *nyoi* (Buddhist implement).

Shuko made a deep bow.

"What are you like when you don't

want to take tea?" Ikkyu demanded.

Without a word, Shuko got up and moved toward the door.

"Stop!" Ikkyu said. "What are you like when you've taken tea?"

Shuko said, "The willow is green, the rose is red."

Ikkyu smiled with pleasure at Shuko's grasp of Zen.

***

Master Fugai, a painter, was a learned and generous master. He was also very strict—with himself and his disciples. Occasionally he would go to live in a

ZEN

mountain cave, where he would medi-tate.

One day, a monk named Bundo, intrigued by Fugai's reputation, called at the cave and asked if the master would put him up for the night. Glad to, the master said.

The next morning, the master made rice gruel for his guest; but since he didn't have an extra bowl, he went out and found a skull lying next to a tomb. How convenient! After return-ing, he filled the skull with gruel and offered it to Bundo.

Bundo, nauseated, looked at the

master as if Fugai had gone crazy. This enraged Fugai, who kicked and punched the monk until he'd driven him from the cave.

"Idiot!" Fugai yelled after the fleeing monk. "With all your vain ideas about filth and purity, how can you call yourself a Buddhist?"

＊

There was a young lord of Osu, in the province of Iyo, who was extremely enthusiastic about the arts of war—perhaps a little too much so. One day, Master Bankei called on this lord. As

the two were sitting face to face, the lord unexpectedly grabbed his spear and jabbed at Bankei.

But the master flicked the spear aside without effort.

"You're too high-strung," he said to the lord.

Years later, when the young lord had grown into a great warrior, he said that Bankei had given him the lesson that mattered the most.

❦

Shan-tao was walking in the mountains with his master, Shih-t'ou, when they came to a turn in the path blocked by the overhanging branches of a tree. The master asked Shan-tao to clear the branches away.

"Oops," Shan-tao said, "I didn't bring my knife."

Shih-t'ou took out his own knife and held it with the blade pointing toward his disciple.

"Um, Master," Shan-tao said, "would you please give me the other end?"

"What do you want to do with the other end?" Shih-t'ou asked.

And Shan-tao woke to the truth of Zen.

Gisan, an extremely severe master,
happened to notice a disciple wiping
his nose because he'd caught a nasty
cold.

"Idiot!" Gisan snapped. "You think
your nose is that important? What a
waste of tissue!"

From then on, the disciple scrupu-
lously avoided using a tissue to wipe
his nose. He also tried not to catch
colds.

In his 1975 book *Powers of Mind,*
which more or less described the emer-

gence of New Age beliefs in America, author Adam Smith included a brief anecdote about a Zen master who happened to be visiting America:

A long line of awed guests had assembled to greet the master, Smith among them. When it came his turn, Smith suddenly was reminded of an old cowboy ballad that seemed to fit the spirit of Zen. So he sang the first verse:

> I eat when I'm hungry
> I drink when I'm dry
> If the sky don't fall on me
> I'll live till I die.

Smith was about to sing the second verse when he remembered it had to do with getting drunk on rye whisky. Deciding this wasn't very Zen, he sang the first verse over again.

"Ah!" the Zen master barked, making Smith jump. "People believe? Believe this song?"

Smith thought about it.

"Not really," he confessed. "They eat when it's breakfast, and again when it's lunch, and a little bell rings for the coffee wagon—"

"Ah," the Zen master said. "So. So."

A DAY IN THE LIFE OF A ZEN MONK

*The shop-boy in front
of the temple-gate
repeats the sutra
which he never
learned.*
—Buddhist Proverb

Though monks are few, they have been crucial to the history of Zen in Asia. Bodhidharma was a monk, after all, as were those who followed him, nurturing the beginnings of Ch'an in China and later introducing the practice into Japan.

In the United States, the funeral rituals and other Zen traditions so vital to the Japanese public are considered less important. The meditation and koans practiced by the monks are what fascinate us, even if a monastery is the last place on earth we'd ever want to live. Why? Allowing for sect variations, a typical day at a monastery goes something like this:

4:00 A.M.	Rising bell
4:15	Incense offering
4:20	Meditation
5:10	Chanting
6:20	Breakfast
7:00	Cleaning
9:00	Lecture or study
10:00	Meditation or labor
11:00	Chanting
11:30	Midday meal
12:00 noon	Free time
1:00	Study or labor

4:00	Meditation
5:00	Evening meal
5:30	Bath
6:30	Free time
7:30	Meditation
9:00	Sleep

Says author Helen Tworkov, "Marine boot camp is the only American experience that has ever been compared to life in a Zen monastery."

ZEN ART

If your practice is good, you may become proud of it. What you do is good, but something more is added to it. Pride is extra. Right effort is to get rid of something extra.
—Shunryu Suzuki

Ink carefully made from pine resin and the soot of burnt pine twigs; this same ink, brushed onto silk in strange curves to become a mountain, monk, or stalking crane; a polished bamboo wand that could be sculpture but instead is a scoop to hold just the right amount of powdered tea; a tiny garden of pebbles, rocks, and moss that, despite its size, seems to describe an entire universe: these, too, are Zen.

By the fourteenth century the educated classes in Japan had adopted not only the philosophy of Zen, as imported from China, but also its artistic impulses.

In China, Zen priests during the Tang dynasty had encouraged the drinking of tea to enhance meditation. The Japanese soon raised this to a spiritual aesthetic: *Chado*, "the way of tea." Other Zen-influenced arts, important in Japan to this very day, are the ink painting (*sumie*) and calligraphy borrowed from the Chinese, flower arrangement, the incense ceremony, and the classical Noh drama. Whatever the medium, Zen art celebrates both beauty and simplicity.

佛身一

普為三

According to some, Chado not only was a powerful influence on Japanese culture in the sixteenth century, but also is a powerful force even today, in a modern nation struggling to keep its unique cultural identity. And the ceremonial serving and drinking of tea—sometimes called, in the West, the tea ceremony—is at the heart of Zen.

According to author Winston King, a monk named Eisai, the twelfth-century founder of the Rinzai school of Zen in Japan, was the first to promote the drinking of bitter green tea, made from stirring powdered tea leaves into a bowl and whipping the mixture into a froth. Eisai believed that tea was good for the health and also helped keep one awake during meditation. Ceremonies were later developed that emphasized tea serving and drinking (sometimes called *Cha-no-yu,* or "hot water for tea") in an atmosphere of deliberately stylized harmony.

Special teahouses were designed by tea masters, with every feature crafted to convey a mood of austere peace— the teahouse itself, the accompanying

ZEN

garden, the path leading to the tea-house from the waiting room, the choice of scroll or flower arrangement to be displayed in a special alcove. Master potters produced special tea bowls, tea caddies, and flower vases. Whisks to beat the tea were made of delicately woven bamboo.

Naturally, tea has found its way into many a Zen koan and anecdote, such as the following well-known story:

The Zen patriarch Joshu, at ease one day in his monastery, noticed a traveling monk who'd stopped to rest a while. Joshu asked, "Have you been here before?"

"Well, yes," the monk said.

Joshu told him, "Have a cup of tea."

Turning to a second monk, also a traveler, Joshu asked the same question but got a different answer. This monk had never been to the monastery before.

Again Joshu said, "Have a cup of tea."

An attendant who had been watching squinted in puzzlement, then asked Joshu, "Why do you say the

ZEN

exact same thing to both men, even though one's been here before and the other hasn't?"

"Attendant!" Joshu said.

"Yes, sir?"

"Have a cup of tea."

Why does the Master say that Buddhism is democratic? Because of this one idea—all living beings have the Buddha Nature and all can become Buddhas. Now, if that isn't totally egalitarian, what is?
—Heng Ch'an

WORDS AND PHRASES

The whole approach to Buddhism is to develop transcendental common sense, seeing things as they are, without magnifying what is or dreaming about what we would like to be.
—Chogyam Trungpa

A ZEN VOCABULARY

Bodhisattva—from the Sanskrit, meaning "enlightened being."

Ch'an—Chinese for "Zen."

Dharma— the teachings of the Buddha. Sanskrit for "law," whether religious, secular, or natural. Often taken to mean the law of karma, the way, or simply pure emptiness.

Dokusan—Japanese term referring to the personal interview between teacher and student. A regular feature of monastic life either dreaded or eagerly anticipated, depending on the student.

Karma—Sanskrit for "cause and

effect": Reap and ye shall sow, even over several lifetimes. In traditional Buddhism, the goal is to get off the karmic treadmill.

Ki—Japanese for "spirit" or "strength."

Koan—generally taken to mean the spiritual riddles masters like to tell students. In a broader sense, all of life is a koan.

Kyosaku—the "encouragement stick" carried around by Zen masters, who are fond of using it to whack students who have dozed off while meditating.

Nirvana—Sanskrit for "extinction," more specifically, extinction of all

desires. In Buddhism, unlike in television commercials, this is considered a good thing.

Roshi—honored teacher.

Satori—enlightenment. In Chinese, *wu*.

Zazen—to sit in meditation.

Zendo—meditation hall.

~

Do not seek the truth. Only cease
to cherish opinions.
—Zen saying

Originally compiled in the late fifteenth century, the first Zen phrase book—*Ku Zoshi*—contained about five thousand quotations taken from Buddhist sutras, the records of Chinese Zen patriarchs, Confucian texts, Taoist writings, and various Chinese poets. As time went on, the book was supplemented.

For those who study koans, a phrase book is a must: From among the many quotations and sayings, a student is expected to choose a "capping phrase" to repeat to his master.

The capping phrase is both a summary of the koan's truth and a demonstration of the student's understanding. Some phrases follow:

Even a good thing isn't as good as nothing.

It can't be swallowed; it can't be spit out.

To admit a thief to be one's child.

A flute with no holes is the most difficult to blow.

Going to hell as fast as an arrow.

Since three men testified about the tortoise, it's a turtle.

Every sound is Buddha's voice.
Every shape is Buddha's shape.

How can the mountain finch know what the wild swan hopes?

Two monkeys are trying to touch the moon in the water.

Astride a blind ass, he pursues a fierce tiger.

ZAZEN
(A Meditation Primer)

*When an ordinary man
attains knowledge, he is a
sage; when a sage attains
understanding, he is an
ordinary man.*
—Zen saying

Most of us are familiar enough with the concept of meditation—we often use the word in a loose sense, to mean the drifting, soothing state of mind we fall into when we sit and listen to a brook, watch the sun set over the water, or otherwise relax quietly by ourselves.

Of course, there are many more formal ways to meditate, such as the repetition of a special word (*mantra*) or the counting of breaths, and the instructions involved can seem not only lengthy and complicated but intimidating as well.

Herewith is a brief primer on Zen meditation. Do it correctly and you may find yourself following in the footsteps of the masters. It might be wise, however, to keep in mind the following advice from Shimano Eido Roshi, abbot of a Zen monastery in New York: "Let your efforts match your expectations."

• Sit on the floor in a half-lotus or full-lotus position, if can—that means not only crossing your legs but also putting one or both feet on top of your thighs. If, like most people, you find this extremely difficult at first, it's okay to kneel or even sit on a chair. Just keep your legs together and your back straight.

• Relax your shoulders, arms, and legs. Keep your hands in your lap, one hand cupped in the palm of the other, thumbs touching. Let go of all tension.

• Keep your eyes open slightly and your gaze directed toward the floor.

• To help keep your mind from wandering, count your breaths from one to ten. (Breathe through your nose!)

Some breaths will be shallow, some deep—no matter, just try to breathe normally. As soon as you realize your thoughts have wandered, bring your attention back to your breath. Don't chastise yourself—just start counting again at one.

• Relax and try to be absolutely still. If you can, maintain your meditation posture for a minimum of twenty minutes.

• Meditate whenever you can. Even five minutes of vigorous zazen is considered worthy practice.

ART CREDIT

page 1-Takuan   page 2-*Lotus and Bamboo in a Bronze Vase*   page 6-Hakuin   page 10-Ch'ien Hsüan   page 11-Takuan   page 19-Nantembo   page 18-Emperor Hui-tsung   page 24-Hakuin   page 25-Hakuin   page 29-Suio   page 33-Ch'en Hung-shou   page 36-*The Miracles of Kannon*   page 41-Sengai   page 44/45-Sengai   page 51-Gocho   page 55-Nobutada   page 58/59-Kegon-Kyo   page 62-*Twelve Symbol Dragon Robe*   page 65-Sansetsu   page 67-Hakuin   page 70-Fugai   page 75-Ryonen
jacket art: Ch'en Shun

Designed and Typeset by Junie Lee